MUMMIES AND SOUND

BY ANTHONY WACHOLTZ • ILLUSTRATED BY CRISTIAN MALLEA

Consultant:
Joanne K. Olson, PhD
Associate Professor, Science Education
Iowa State University
Ames, Iowa

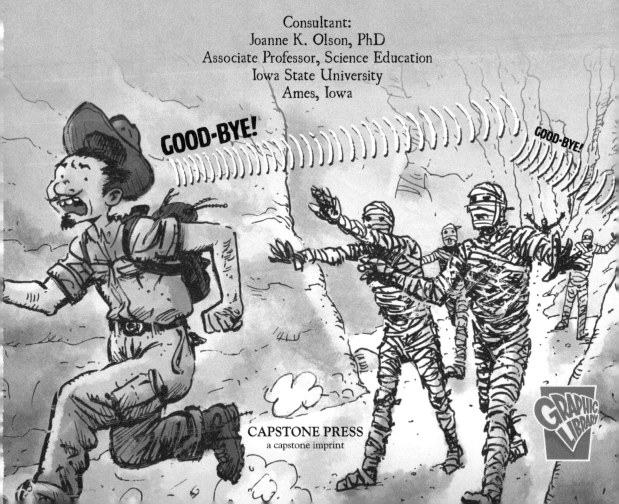

CAPSTONE PRESS
a capstone imprint

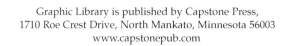

Graphic Library is published by Capstone Press,
1710 Roe Crest Drive, North Mankato, Minnesota 56003
www.capstonepub.com

Library of Congress Cataloging-in-Publication Data
Wacholtz, Anthony.
  Mummies and sound / by Anthony Wacholtz ; illustrated by Cristian Mallea.
    pages cm.—(Graphic library. Monster science)
  Summary: "In cartoon format, uses mummies to explain the science of sound"—Provided by publisher.
  Audience: Grade 4 to 6.
  Includes bibliographical references and index.
  ISBN 978-1-4296-9930-3 (library binding)
  ISBN 978-1-62065-818-5 (paperback)
  ISBN 978-1-4765-3450-3 (eBook PDF)
1. Sound—Juvenile literature. 2. Sound—Comic books, strips, etc. 3. Graphic novels. I. Mallea, Cristian, illustrator. II. Title.
  QC225.5.W28 2014
  534–dc23   2013003112

Editor
Christopher L. Harbo

Designer
Alison Thiele

Art Director
Nathan Gassman

Production Specialist
Laura Manthe

Printed in the United States 5989

TABLE OF
CONTENTS

CHAPTER 1

WHAT IS SOUND?

If you listen closely, you can hear sounds in even the quietest places on Earth.

UUUUUH!

Buzzards cry out as they search for their next meals.

SQUAAAWK!

UUUUUH!

Sand skitters across the dunes in gusts of wind.

UUUUUH!

SKRRTCH

Low moans rise from the depths of the pyramids.

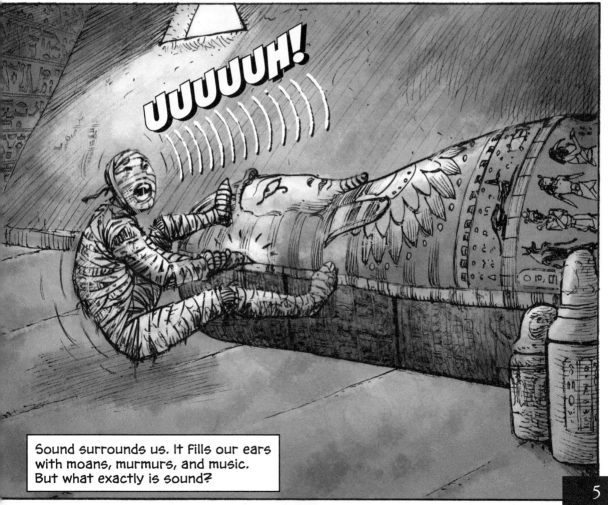

Sound surrounds us. It fills our ears with moans, murmurs, and music. But what exactly is sound?

Sound, like light and heat, is a form of energy.

SIZZLE!

... AND IN OTHER NEWS ...

Energy is the ability to do work. Without energy, plants couldn't grow, fires couldn't burn, and mummies couldn't do ... whatever mummies do.

Sound starts when an object, such as a bell, vibrates. The bell's vibrations cause the molecules in the air around it to vibrate too. The vibrating air molecules push into each other, and sound is created.

molecule—the atoms making up the smallest unit of a substance

Like light, sound travels in waves. Sound waves move outward from the point of the first vibrations.

HELLO???

SOUND SPEED

Sound is a slowpoke compared to light. Sound moves at about 767 miles (1,230 kilometers) per hour. Light, which moves at a whopping 700 million miles (1.1 billion km) per hour, leaves sound in the dust!

LIGHT

SOUND

CHAPTER 2

PICKING APART SOUND

All sounds travel in waves. But sounds differ in many ways. Some are soft, while others are loud. For example, mummies can moan softly, but they can also let out a frightening wail.

The loudness of a sound depends on how much the air molecules vibrate. Strong vibrations create loud sounds. Weak vibrations make quieter sounds.

The difference in the loudness of a sound is called volume.

AAAA-CHOOO!

A high-volume sound is loud, and a low-volume sound is soft.

AAAAAH!

AH, MUCH BETTER.

BANDAGES

DECIBELS

The volume of a sound is measured in decibels. A motorcycle is 10 decibels higher and 10 times louder than a ringing phone. A lawn mower is 20 decibels higher than a ringing phone, but it's 100 times louder. Fireworks are a whopping 1 trillion times louder than a whisper!

volume—the measure of how loud something is
decibel—a unit for measuring the volume of sounds

Sound isn't just about how loud a mummy can wail. A sound's frequency and pitch are important too.

HERE'S THE PITCH.

No, not that kind of pitch.

frequency—the number of sound waves that pass a location in a certain amount of time

pitch—the highness or lowness of a sound; low pitches have low frequencies and high pitches have high frequencies

Let's start with frequency. Imagine a line of mummies waiting to see a movie. The line represents a sound, and each mummy stands for a sound wave. The number of mummies that pass through the door over a certain period of time is the sound's frequency.

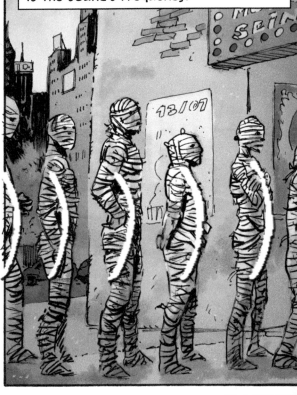

A sound has a low frequency if its waves are far apart.

A high-frequency sound has waves that are close together.

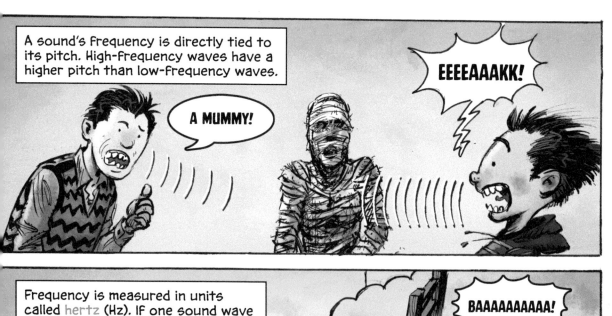

A sound's frequency is directly tied to its pitch. High-frequency waves have a higher pitch than low-frequency waves.

A MUMMY!

EEEEAAAKK!

Frequency is measured in units called hertz (Hz). If one sound wave passes a certain point each second, the frequency would be 1 Hz.

BAAAAAAAAAA!

1 HERTZ

hertz—a unit for measuring the frequency of sound waves; one hertz equals one sound wave per second

WHAT HAPPENS IF A SOUND HAS A REALLY HIGH FREQUENCY, LIKE THE NOISE FROM THAT DOG WHISTLE?

Humans can only hear sounds with frequencies between 20 and 20,000 Hz. Dogs have super-human hearing. They can hear sounds up to 40,000 Hz!

IT REALLY HERTZ!

CHAPTER 3

SOUND ON THE MOVE

As sound waves travel, they're bound to come across some obstacles along the way. What happens to the sound waves depends on the surfaces they hit.

Soft surfaces absorb sound waves.

If a sound wave reaches a hard surface, the surface absorbs some of the sound. The rest of the sound reflects off the surface.

absorb—to soak up
reflect—to bounce off an object

We hear a sound more than once if the sound reflects off hard surfaces. That's called an echo.

But sound doesn't bounce around forever. Over time, it loses its energy, and the echo fades away.

The direction a reflected sound wave takes depends on the angle and texture of the surface it hits.

YOU SHOULD SEE THE VIEW FROM UP HERE!

HEY! GET DOWN FROM THERE!

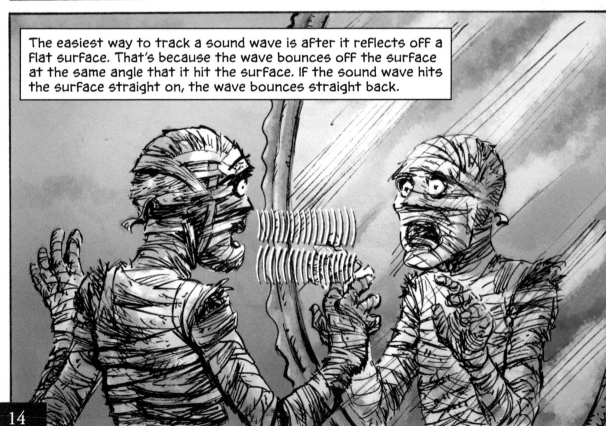

The easiest way to track a sound wave is after it reflects off a flat surface. That's because the wave bounces off the surface at the same angle that it hit the surface. If the sound wave hits the surface straight on, the wave bounces straight back.

Imagine two mummies bouncing a ball to each other. If the ball hits the ground at a 45-degree angle, it springs forward at a 45-degree angle. Likewise, any sound waves that hit an object at a 45-degree angle will bounce off it at the same angle.

Things can get bumpy on a surface that isn't flat. Rough surfaces cause the sound waves to bounce off in many directions. A rough surface also absorbs more of the sound.

Air isn't the only thing sound travels through. It also moves through solids and liquids.

SOUND TRAVELS THROUGH SOLIDS. MUMMIES DO NOT.

WHUMP!

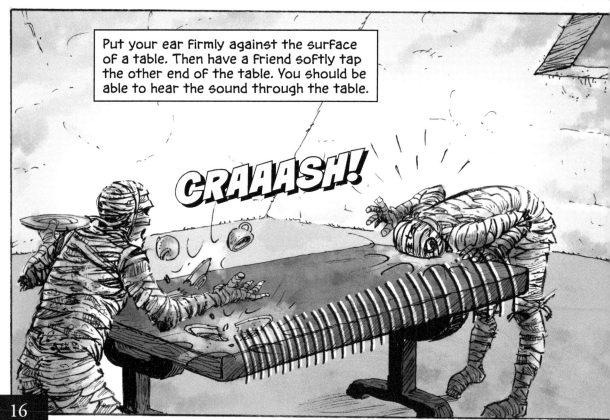

Put your ear firmly against the surface of a table. Then have a friend softly tap the other end of the table. You should be able to hear the sound through the table.

CRAAASH!

SOUND IN SPACE?

Sound can only travel by sending waves through substances, like air, water, or a wall. But if there is no substance, there is nothing to vibrate and carry the waves. Outer space is a vacuum, which means that it has no air, or any molecules at all. If you tried to talk in outer space, no one would hear you.

refract—to bend when passing through a material at an angle
vacuum—a space that has no air or other matter in it

Temperature also plays a role in how fast sound moves. Sound moves faster in hot temperatures. Heat causes molecules to vibrate faster, which speeds up the sound waves.

OUCH!

BBBRRRR!

On the other hand, cold temperatures make it harder for sound to get around. Without much heat, the molecules slow down. The slower vibrations lead to slower sound waves.

FASTER THAN SOUND

When something moves faster than the speed of sound, it's called breaking the sound barrier. Sound waves build up and create a loud sound. That's what happens when you crack a whip or when a supersonic jet produces a deafening boom.

BOOM!

CHAPTER 4

MAKING SOUND, HEARING SOUND

Sounds come from many different sources. One of the most familiar sounds—your voice—starts in the throat.

SAY AAAAH!

AAAAH!

The throat contains an organ called the larynx. Inside the larynx are vocal cords. These two muscles control the flow of air through the larynx.

LARYNX

organ—a part of the body that does a certain job

As air passes by the vocal cords, they come together and vibrate. The vibrations create your voice.

The way your vocal cords vibrate affects how high or low your voice sounds. Vocal cords that vibrate quickly create a high-pitched voice.

I·I·I'M GONNA BE SI·I·I·CK!

As the sounds leave your throat, you use your mouth and tongue to form words.

DO·RE·MI·FA·SO·LA·TI·DO!

LARYNGITIS

If you spend a lot of time screaming, you might end up with laryngitis. Your vocal cords become swollen and are unable to vibrate as much. If that happens, your voice will sound hoarse or you won't be able to talk.

HE LOST HIS VOICE. IT MUST BE AROUND HERE SOMEWHERE.

After leaving the mouth, sound makes its way to our ears. Let's take a closer look at how ears work.

IF A MUMMY FALLS IN THE FOREST, DOES HE MAKE A SOUND?

WAAAAA!

To hear a sound, your ear has to be able to "catch" the noise first. The outer part of your ear, called the pinna, is shaped to do just that. The pinna funnels in sound waves from all directions. The curves of your ear don't just catch sounds. They also help you figure out where the sounds are coming from.

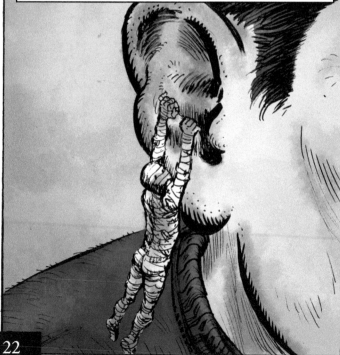

After the sound waves enter your outer ear, they travel down the ear canal and into the middle ear.

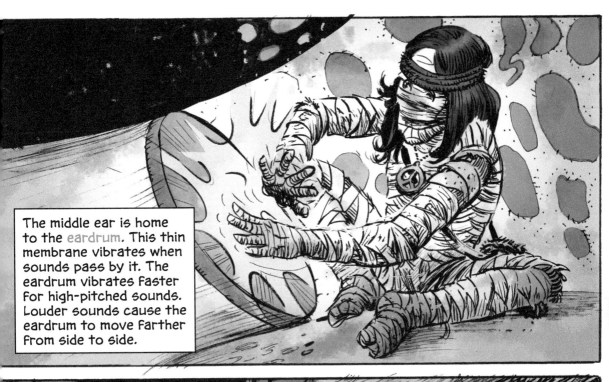

The middle ear is home to the eardrum. This thin membrane vibrates when sounds pass by it. The eardrum vibrates faster for high-pitched sounds. Louder sounds cause the eardrum to move farther from side to side.

When the eardrum vibrates, it moves three tiny bones called the hammer, anvil, and stirrup. The bones increase the volume of the sounds before they pass to the inner ear.

STIRRUP

ANVIL

HAMMER

INNER EAR

eardrum—a thin piece of skin stretched tight like a drum inside the ear; the eardrum vibrates when sound waves strike it

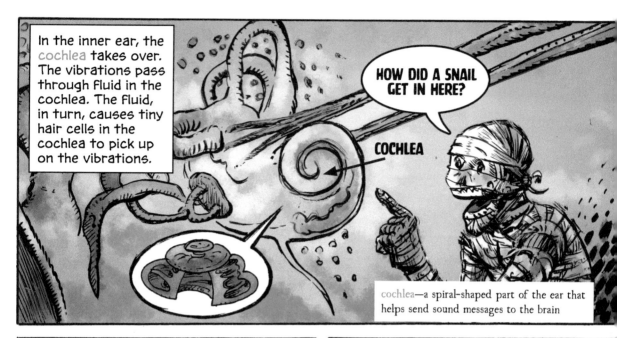

In the inner ear, the cochlea takes over. The vibrations pass through fluid in the cochlea. The fluid, in turn, causes tiny hair cells in the cochlea to pick up on the vibrations.

HOW DID A SNAIL GET IN HERE?

COCHLEA

cochlea—a spiral-shaped part of the ear that helps send sound messages to the brain

When the hair cells have the information they need, they send signals to the brain. The brain uses the signals to figure out what the sounds are.

BARK WOOF RUFF

HMMM ... WHAT COULD HE BE HEARING?

All the parts of your ear work together so you can hear. But sometimes noises can be so loud that they damage your ear.

HE LOCKED HIS KEYS IN THERE AGAIN.

Loud noises can damage or kill the hair cells in the ear. When the hair cells stop working properly, the ear can't send signals to the brain.

NO PROBLEM. THEY JUST NEED SOME WATER.

Actually, these hair cells don't grow back.

If the hair cells become damaged, there is a way to boost hearing. A hearing aid helps the damaged hair cells so they can still do their job.

WHERE ARE THIS GUY'S EARS???

DR. M/W

TRACKING SOUNDS

You can tell which direction a sound comes from because your ears are on opposite sides of your head. But because they are at the same height, it's hard to tell the height of the sound's source. For example, you might hear a bird chirping in a tree. But it would be hard for you to tell the height of the bird. Some animals, such as dogs, tilt their heads so that their ears are at different heights. That helps them better locate the sound.

CHIRP!

CHAPTER 5

SOUND ALL AROUND

Once people learned how sound works, they started finding ways to use it. In 1876 Alexander Graham Bell invented the first telephone. The device changed sounds into electric signals. The signals passed through a wire, and then they changed back to sounds.

IS YOUR REFRIGERATOR RUNNING?

YES?

THEN YOU'D BETTER CATCH IT!

Cell phones work the same way but without the wires. Cell phones transmit sound through the air as radio waves.

NO SERVICE ... AGAIN?!

Another way sound has changed the world is through music. Musical instruments allow us to create beautiful sounds.

For instance, an acoustic guitar makes sound when you pluck the strings. The strings vibrate the front of the guitar. When the front of the guitar vibrates, the air inside the guitar starts to vibrate as well. With nowhere else to go, the vibrating air comes out the guitar's sound hole.

It would be tough to keep the beat without the sound from a drum. When a drummer slams down with a drumstick, the face of the drum vibrates. The sound that pulses from the drum depends on where the drum face is struck.

Speakers create sound by changing electric signals into vibrations. The vibrations come out of the speaker as music and other sounds.

Humans aren't the only ones getting the most out of sound. Animals use sounds every day.

RAWWWR!

CHIRP!

MOOOOO!

BAAARK!

SQUAWK!

From chirping and barking to mooing and roaring, many animals use sound to communicate. Animals share food, find mates, scare off predators, and claim territory through sound.

LET'S FIND ANOTHER SPOT.

Rattlesnakes use sound to ward off predators. Their tails shake like rattles when they are threatened.

RATTLE

THIS ISN'T SO SCARY.

The loud noises let predators know they'd better steer clear.

Animals such as dolphins use sonar to help them move. A dolphin sends out sound waves underwater. These waves bounce off objects and back to the dolphin. The dolphin senses the returning sound wave and knows something is in its way.

BAM!

sonar—the ability to send sound waves through water and listen for when they bounce back off something

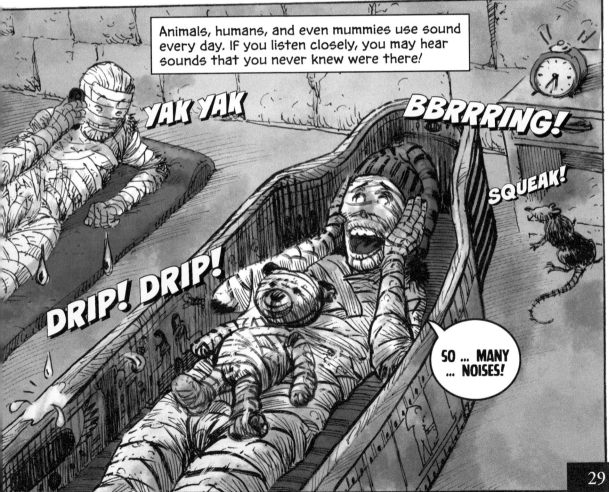

Animals, humans, and even mummies use sound every day. If you listen closely, you may hear sounds that you never knew were there!

YAK YAK

BBRRRING!

SQUEAK!

DRIP! DRIP!

SO ... MANY ... NOISES!

GLOSSARY

absorb (ab-ZORB)—to soak up

cochlea (KOH-klee-uh)—a spiral-shaped part of the ear that helps send sound messages to the brain

decibel (DEH-suh-buhl)—a unit for measuring the volume of sounds

eardrum (EER-druhm)—a thin piece of skin stretched tight like a drum inside the ear; the eardrum vibrates when sound waves strike it

frequency (FREE-kwuhn-see)—the number of sound waves that pass a location in a certain amount of time

hertz (HURTS)—a unit for measuring the frequency of sound waves; one hertz equals one sound wave per second

molecule (MOL-uh-kyool)—the atoms making up the smallest unit of a substance

organ (OR-guhn)—a part of the body that does a certain job

pitch (PICH)—the highness or lowness of a sound; low pitches have low frequencies and high pitches have high frequencies

reflect (ri-FLEKT)—to bounce off an object

refract (ri-FRACT)—to bend when passing through a material at an angle

sonar (SOH-nar)—the ability to send sound waves through water and listen for when they bounce back off something

vacuum (VAK-yoom)—a space that has no air or other matter in it

vibration (vye-BRAY-shuhn)—a fast movement back and forth

volume (VOL-yuhm)—the measure of how loud something is

CRITICAL THINKING USING THE COMMON CORE

1. Why does the Sphinx's nose fall off in the top panel of page 9? What does this action tell you about the sound coming from the mummy? (Key Ideas and Details)

2. What is the relationship between the frequency and pitch of a sound? In the top panel of page 11, which character's voice has a lower pitch and why? (Key Ideas and Details)

3. Through what type of material does sound travel the fastest? Explain how and why it is possible for sound to travel at different speeds through different materials. (Integration of Knowledge and Ideas)

READ MORE

Brasch, Nicolas. *Why Does Sound Travel?: All about Sound.* Solving Science Mysteries. New York: PowerKids Press, 2010.

Claybourne, Anna. *The Science of a Guitar: The Science of Sound.* The Science of. Pleasantville, N.Y.: Gareth Stevens Publishing, 2009.

Kessler, Colleen. *A Project Guide to Sound.* Physical Science Projects for Kids. Hockessin, Del.: Mitchell Lane, 2012.

INTERNET SITES

FactHound offers a safe, fun way to find Internet sites related to this book. All sites on FactHound have been researched by our staff.

Here's all you do:

Visit *www.facthound.com*

Type in this code: 9781429699303

 Check out projects, games and lots more at **www.capstonekids.com**

INDEX